Sulgrave  M

The Northamptonshire home of   *George Washington's ancestors*

You are now standing on American and British soil. Sulgrave Manor is unique in that it belongs equally to both sovereign nations, hence the flag of each country flying in the grounds.

This superb example of a manor house and garden dating from 1539, and the home of the ancestors of George Washington, was presented to the Peoples of Great Britain and the United States of America, in celebration of the Hundred Years Peace between the two nations. The special relationship between this very English house and the government and people of the United States continues to this day. Today visitors from all over the world, including many schoolchildren, come to enjoy this beautiful Tudor house set within the heart of a peaceful Northamptonshire village.

Tour of the Manor

The House & Gardens

Tour of the Manor

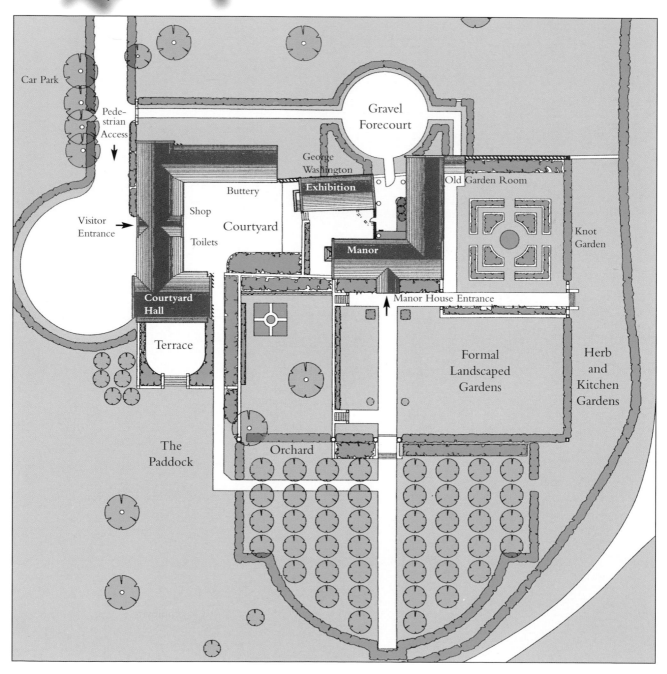

Car Park

Pede-strian Access

Visitor Entrance

Gravel Forecourt

George Washington

Old Garden Room

Buttery

Exhibition

Knot Garden

Shop

Courtyard

Toilets

Manor

Courtyard Hall

Manor House Entrance

Terrace

Formal Landscaped Gardens

Herb and Kitchen Gardens

The Paddock

Orchard

The Courtyard and Courtyard Hall

On the 8th of April 1999 the new Courtyard range of buildings was opened by Lord Hurd of Westwell.

Funded with the assistance of a considerable grant from the Heritage Lottery Fund, this £1.1 million complex gives the Manor wonderful Visitor and Education facilities. The Buttery provides a delightful setting for a variety of refreshments; the new shop a superb range of gifts, mementoes and souvenirs; the traditionally timbered and galleried Courtyard Hall allows us to expand our educational programmes as well as providing a perfect venue for a host of events, exhibitions and functions. Do ask for our brochure for private hire.

Designed round a beautifully sheltered Courtyard these new facilities completely complement and enhance the visitor experience. The materials used, the craftsmanship employed and the sympathetic siting in relation to the original Tudor Manor House, make the whole a complete triumph!

The Porch and Screens Passage

The visitor enters the house through the porch. On one side of this entrance-way is a huge representation in pargeting of the lion of England and on the other of the dragon of Wales. Both taken from the Arms of Elizabeth on the front of the Porch and in such a position virtually unique.

On one side of the passage is an oak screen, a reproduction of one which would have divided the Great Hall from the Screens Passage, beyond which once lay the kitchen and buttery in the old west wing.

At the end of this passage is a copy of the well-known bust of George Washington by Houdon

Salt cupboard, showing the
initials of Lawrence Washington
and the five pointed star that
became the symbol of the USA.

The Great Hall

The Great Hall, a large bare room, has a floor of
blue Hornton stone. When the Manor was restored, not only had a
mid–19th century brick partition to be removed, but also plaster from the
ceiling, revealing fine oak beams; and a modern grate, disclosing the open
Tudor fireplace. The form of the ceiling gives an indication of the age of
the building, but in the course of restoration added evidence appeared,
for in a crevice between the ceiling and the roof of the floor
above there were discovered objects which we can be sure
date from the days of the builder: a silver
Elizabethan sixpence of 1568, an Elizabethan
baby's shoe (right), now in the Deed Room, and a
knife and case (below), of a quality and
decoration which indicate that they
belonged to Lawrence
Washington himself.

Single-handed
Lantern clock
c.1600 by John
Smith of Derby

The chimney opening is 7' 2" wide and 4' 5" high, the depth of the embrasure being 2' 8". On a cold night it was possible to sit within this open fireplace. The original oak chimney seat is on the left, with a small niche in the wall conveniently near to hold a mug of ale.

The furniture in this room, including the oak refectory table in the centre, the dresser beneath the Peale portrait, the settle against the north wall and the rare child's chair by the fireplace, are original pieces, chosen as being typical of their period. This applies to the furniture throughout the house.

*17th century
child's chair*

*The oak hanging
dole cupboard against
the north wall is
beautifully decorated
with carving and
geometrical inlay in
holly and bog oak.
It was once used to
house bread and ale
which was given to
passing strangers and
travellers who formally
asked for the 'dole'*

Coat of Arms of Robert Washington of Warton in Lancashire, second son of his father, thus the crescent as a heraldic mark for difference

Marital shield celebrating the marriage of the builder's father, John Washington of Warton and Margaret Kytson, sister of Sir Thomas Kytson of Hengrave, Suffolk (the ancestor of Earl Spencer and Sir Winston Churchill)

Marital shield celebrating the second marriage of Lawrence Washington, the builder of Sulgrave Manor to Amy Pargiter, daughter of Robert Pargiter of Greatworth, the next parish to Sulgrave

The windows contain reproductions in stained glass of the arms of members of the Washington family; four of the originals are in Fawsley Church just eight miles from Sulgrave, and the others are in the Corning Glass Museum in the United States. These original panels are known to have been in the windows of the kitchen in the eighteenth century. In the large window are the arms of the builder's grandfather; of his parents; his own; and of his eldest son. In the small window are those of the builder's second son and of his grand-daughter. The last is dated 1588, and probably all the original panels date from then, having been ordered by Robert Washington in celebration of his eldest son's marriage.

Above the fireplace hangs the most valued object in the house, an original portrait in oils of George Washington by Gilbert Stuart, the greatest of American portrait painters. He made a number of such paintings of Washington. This one was commissioned by Chief Justice Shippen and was for long in the possession of his family.

On the south wall Washington is seen as a colonel commanding the Virginian Colonial Troops. This is a copy of the painting executed by Charles Willson Peale in 1772, the original of which is at Washington and Lee University in Virginia. The carved gilt frame is after a design by Paul Revere, the hero of the famous midnight ride to rouse the Minute Men at the start of the American Revolution. He was also a well-known silversmith.

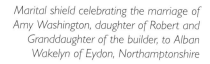

Detail of the carved gilt frame after a design by Paul Revere

Marital shield celebrating the first marriage of Robert Washington, the builder's eldest son and heir to Elizabeth Light, daughter of Walter Light of Radway Grange, Warwickshire

Marital shield celebrating the marriage of Lawrence Washington, the second son of the builder and Martha Newce, daughter of Clement Newce of Great Hadham, Hertfordshire

Marital shield celebrating the marriage of Amy Washington, daughter of Robert and Granddaughter of the builder, to Alban Wakelyn of Eydon, Northamptonshire

George Washington
First President of the
United States of America

by Gilbert Stuart

The Oak Parlour

The circular mahogany tripod tea-table on which is laid out a blue and white Salopian teaset c. 1730

We now leave the original Washington Manor, to enter the 18th century wing built by John Hodges after the Washington family had emigrated to America. This small room, with its fine panelling, dates from about 1700, somewhat later than the Charles II staircase which runs from the small hall adjoining it. During the nineteenth century its walls, like those of the Great Hall, were covered with wallpaper, and its elm flooring covered with Hornton stone over which modern floorboards were placed.

The lacquered grandfather clock is by Thomas Utting of Yarmouth. The wooden dummy of a small boy shows the style of dress of a child about 1690; such pieces are rare. The Queen Anne walnut settee is covered with contemporary petit point needlework. The spinet,

of walnut inlaid with sycamore, dates from about 1710 and is the work of Thomas Hitchcock. Its folding book-rest is an especially rare feature for an instrument of that date. On it rests a fine copy of a music book dated 1747, called '*Lessons for the Harpsichord*'. Among the list of subscribers which is bound into the volume is the name of Handel. Above the settee hangs a portrait in oils of George Washington painted in 1792 by the Scottish painter, Archibald Robertson, for the eleventh Earl of Buchan (see page 25). During the nineteenth century it was lost. Only in recent years was it re-identified, and presented to the Manor.

The Oak Parlour showing the lacquered grandfather clock by Thomas Utting and either side of the fireplace, two walnut chairs with typical Queen Anne spoon backs

Opposite: The Hitchcock Spinet in the Oak Parlour dating from 1730

The Great Kitchen

Unlike the other rooms in the house, the kitchen was not furnished piecemeal. At the time the Manor was being restored, the opportunity was taken to acquire in its entirety the two hundred-year-old kitchen, with all its fittings and equipment, of a manor house at Weston Corbett in Hampshire.

Sulgrave Manor regularly holds events and days when history is recreated and visitors can enjoy the spectacle of seeing the manor and its rooms as they would have appeared during the Tudor and Elizabethan periods.

The fireplace contains three ovens, one a charcoal brazier, whose wrought-iron top was used for heating flat-irons. When the brazier was not alight, its top could be used as a seat, for which there is a niche in the wall. Secondly, there is an iron-lined oven on which the whole of the kitchen fire was placed. The logs were arranged with their ends resting on two small fire-dogs, which had an iron bar across them to prevent them from falling out. This oven could also be heated from below, by placing hot ashes in a brick-lined channel which runs from a trap-door in the hearth to the back of the fireplace. The top of the oven could be used as a hot-plate; the interior chiefly for making pastry, but also for keeping food hot and plates warm. The third oven, lined with fireproof brick, was mainly used for the baking of bread.

Detail of an Elizabethan Belamine jug

Tudor scales for weighing spices and herbs

Meat was roasted on a spit; by Elizabethan times this was turned, quite slowly, by mechanical means, a weight on a chain passing over a cogwheel attached to another such wheel. The weight used could be varied with the size of the joint to be roasted, which was stuck through by a meat-spit. This kitchen contains spits of four different sizes. From the great potcrane, with a swinging arm six feet long, could be suspended pot-hooks, on which pots could be hung at any distance from the fire desired. Extending round the fireplace in a semi-circle near the ceiling is an iron rod, from which curtains hung. When drawn, enclosing a space round the fireplace, they would provide some defence against draughts. As short curtains they would also have been used to assist in controlling the fire.

The intricate mechanics of the spit

The White Bedroom

The canopied four-post bedstead is covered with ancient material in a conventional design. This small room, like the Chintz Bedroom beside it, contains items of furniture which would be found in rooms of the Queen Anne period in a house of this standing.

Here again is an example of child's furniture: a baby-walker or cage (right), the equivalent of the modern 'pen', but with the addition of a tray for food. This served not only to help the child to learn to walk but also to contain him in a particular place.

Walnut firescreen, with a brightly coloured picture in petit-point of a shepherd and shepherdess with sheep and dogs

Note also the embroidered white waistcoat and the shoes by the bed; both of the period

The Chintz Bedroom

The four-post bedstead in this room is upholstered with Queen Anne linen delicately embroidered in crimson and blue.

The coverlet, like that in the White Bedroom, is finely quilted. The most important piece of furniture here is the carved and painted mahogany chair with back of Hepplewhite design, made about 1790, which belonged once to George Washington. Notice also the portable or travelling spinning wheel with flax *in situ*.

Glazed bust of George Washington in coloured Staffordshire ware

A detail of George Washington's chair taken prior to its restoration

The Great Chamber

This room, almost 18 feet square, is floored with extraordinarily wide slabs of polished oak. The high-pitched, double-framed roof is impressively solid. To the left of the fireplace, over what is now a wall-cupboard, is an early beam, once a doorway leading to a room in the east wing which no longer exists. It is the fireplace of this room which can

be seen from outside. It was of precisely the same size and design as the fireplace of the Great Chamber, which backs on to it.

Detail of exquisitely embroidered Stuart stump-work toilet mirror. Another of the great treasures of the house

The canopied four-post bedstead is Elizabethan and came from Battle Abbey in Sussex. The carving of the back of the cornice and the bedposts is uniformly fine and immensely varied. Note, as in the case of other important Elizabethan bedsteads, the 'bedstock' – the part supporting the mattress – stands clear of the bedposts. Near the bed stands an Elizabethan chest, carved with palm leaves on the four uprights and lions' masks on the panels, one of the rarest pieces in the house.

The Elizabethan Embroidery Project

The New Elizabethan Embroidery project is an eight-year project launched in 1995 to create a hand-stitched sixteenth century style textile for the Elizabethan carved oak canopied bed in the Great Bedchamber. Individual embroidered motifs, 'slips' of forty different designs, are being stitched by volunteers across the United Kingdom and the United States of America. They will be decoratively applied to green velvet to make new bed hangings. An upper valance depicting the story of the Washington family is also planned.

The smaller chest at the foot of the bed is carved to illustrate Nonesuch, Henry VIII's palace which was pulled down in the reign of Charles I. Here also are interesting examples of children's furniture: a baby's high-backed chair and a cradle.

The tapestry on the north wall dates from the seventeenth century. Nearby, in a window, is the coat of arms of Robert Washington in Elizabethan glass (right).

The Deed Room and Porch Room

These two small rooms, used as a museum, contain such relics of George Washington as his saddle-bags, his velvet coat (right), his oak liquor-chest and a lock of his hair. There are a number of portraits of him, including several good miniatures in various forms and silhouettes. The pearwood snuff-box, presented by HM Queen Mary was made at the beginning of the nineteenth century, but the design, showing Washington in profile, and the inscription, date from about 1777. There are a number of most interesting autographed letters in this room.

Pearwood snuff-box showing Washington in profile.

Handle of the coffin of George Washington

The Washington Gavel made from maplewood and bound with silver belonging to 'Wakefield', the Virginia birthplace of George

Among the rarest objects here is an engraved Peace Medal of silver. Such medals were given by the President to friendly Indian chiefs. One side shows Washington and an Indian chief exchanging a pipe of peace, the other shows the eagle of the newly formed republic.

Only a small proportion of the many deeds relating to the Manor which the Sulgrave Manor Board possesses can be displayed. The one dated 1606 (right), shows the signatures of Robert Washington, the builder's eldest son, and of Robert's sons, Robert and Lawrence.

Miniatures of George Washington and his wife in ivory painted frames

The House and Gardens

The Gardens

One of the most attractive features of the Manor is its grounds. To the east is the knot-garden, in the centre of which has been placed a sundial dating from 1579. Around this, lavender flourishes and many thousands of bags of Sulgrave lavender have crossed the Atlantic since the house was opened. On either side of the porch are herbaceous borders, and stretching southwards is the well-kept lawn with its fine topiary work. A path across this lawn leads to the orchard. The lawn is bordered on the west by a wall made from materials which came in the first instance from parts of the Tudor house which were destroyed. On the terrace beneath this wall fly the Union Jack and the Stars and Stripes.

Top right: View of the South Front and New Courtyard Hall from the east

Right: Re-enactors in the Paddock

Bottom right: The South Entrance porch with its intriguing armorials

Below, the 'Lady' of the House chats to her staff in the North Courtyard

Elizabethan clay pipe found in the garden at the Manor

Sulgrave Manor

Sulgrave Manor is a small manor-house, built by a Lancashireman born at Warton about 1500. His ancestry, and the family name, can be traced back to the manor of Wessington in County Durham about the end of the twelfth century.

Lawrence Washington himself left Warton, where he was employed by Sir William Parr, uncle of Henry VIII's last Queen, and moved in 1529 to Northamptonshire, where Parr had large interests. However he soon left his employ when he discovered that his cousin, John Spencer of Althorp was making a singular fortune out of the wool trade. At about this time he married Elizabeth Gough, the young widow of a rich aged woolstapler of the town of Northampton. There is no doubt that he had befriended the said William Gough and this union had been arranged between them. He flourished sufficiently as a wool merchant to become Mayor in 1532. His first wife died in childbirth, the most common form of death for a woman in

Tudor times. He then married another widow, Amy Tomson, daughter of Robert Pargiter of Greatworth, a neighbouring village to Sulgrave. It was through this marriage that Lawrence acquired the lease to the Manor of Sulgrave.

Memorial brasses, from the Church of St James the Less in Sulgrave, to Lawrence Washington's children showing the four sons (above), and seven daughters (right)

The opportunity fell to him in 1539, at the dissolution of the monasteries, to purchase it outright from the Crown for the sum of £324 – 14s – 10d. The Manor had belonged to the Priory of St Andrew at Northampton. By his second wife Amy, Lawrence was to have four sons and seven daughters. To accommodate this expanding family, and to enable him to administer his increasingly prosperous wool business (he was Mayor of Northampton again in 1545), Lawrence built the house, the remaining parts of which are seen by visitors today.

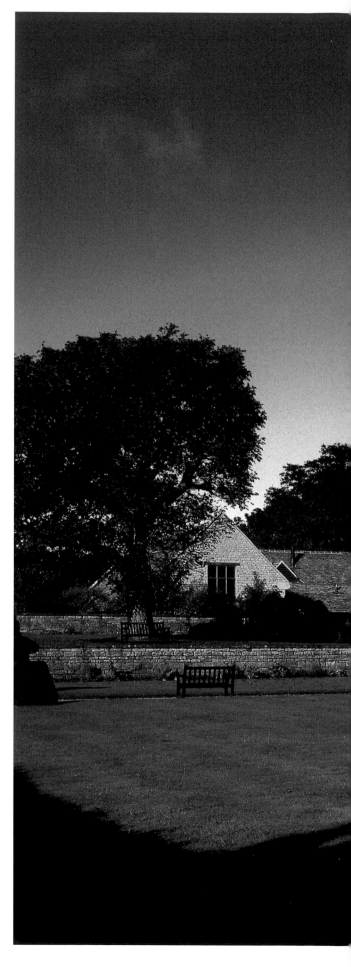

The date at which the house was completed can be fixed by architectural evidence at about 1560; Lawrence survived until 1584. His eldest son Robert continued to live in the house until his death in 1619, and for six years after that it was occupied by Robert's widow Anne. Meanwhile however, in 1601, Robert had transferred actual ownership of the house to his eldest son, Lawrence; and while his father was still living there, in 1610, Lawrence sold the reversion of it to his cousin Lawrence Makepeace, the son of the builder's daughter Mary. He took up residence in 1626, and the Makepeaces retained it until 1659, so that the house was in the ownership of the builder's family for almost a century after its building was completed. In 1656, three years before the Makepeaces disposed of the house, John Washington, grandson of the Lawrence who sold it to them and son of the Rev. Lawrence Washington, emigrated to Virginia.

We may conjecture whether he did so for business reasons or otherwise; but it is not unreasonable to suppose that he was discouraged by the treatment meted out to his father during the Civil War between Charles I and Parliament. The Rev. Lawrence Washington had strong royalist affiliations. His brother Sir William Washington, was brother-in-law of the King's favourite, George Villiers, Duke of Buckingham. Another brother, Thomas, had been page to the King on his voyage to Madrid in 1623. Yet another, Sir John Washington was a prominent royalist; and Sir William's son, Colonel Henry Washington, actually held Worcester for the King and fought for him at Edgehill in 1642. The Rev. Lawrence Washington was ousted from the good living he held at Purleigh in Essex in 1643 and eked out a meagre existence thereafter. England, therefore, was no healthy climate for a man with John's family connections. Thus he left for Virginia in 1656.

His son, yet another Lawrence, and his grandson Augustine paid temporary visits to England. But the family's settlement in Virginia was permanent. There in 1732, was born John's great-grandson George, first President of the United States; and there he died, childless, in 1799.

This portrait of George Washington by Archibald Robertson, can be seen in the Oak Parlour

It will be seen that George's direct ancestors had played no very prominent part in the history of England, although some members of the family attained distinction as soldiers and lawyers.

The builder's second son, Lawrence, became Registrar of the Court of Chancery, and so did his son, also called Lawrence, who was knighted. But the family fortunes were firmly based in the first instance on wool. Lawrence the builder, besides his connection with Sir William Parr, had family ties with Sir Thomas Kytson of Hengrave Hall and with the still more important Spencer family of Althorp, not far from Sulgrave. Both Lawrence and his eldest son, Robert, made acquisitions of land. Robert's son, Lawrence, became tenant, and possibly agent, of his Spencer kinsman, and

was buried at Great Brington, the village nearest Althorp. He was born at Sulgrave, as was also his son, the Rev. Lawrence Washington. John, the emigrant, is thought to have been born about 1632, when his father was still Rector of Purleigh and the Manor in the occupation of the Makepeaces. Edward Plant, who had bought the house in 1659, retained it for only fourteen years, and it then passed into the hands of The Rev. Moses Hodges. John Hodges, his son, consolidated the lands around the house, uniting for the first time all three of the mediaeval manors into which it had previously been divided; Lawrence Makepeace had added one of these to the St. Andrew's manor during his ownership. John Hodges it was also who did much of the rebuilding which gives the house the shape it has today. The descendants of Moses and John Hodges remained owners, but not invariably occupiers, of the house until 1840. It had already become much dilapidated by the end of the eighteenth century. Before its sale in 1840 to The Hon. Henry Hely-Hutchinson of Weston, the neighbouring parish, it had been described as a common farmhouse. From him it passed to Lt.-Col. Arthur Reynell-Pack and, on his death in 1860, to Mr. Arthur Reynell Pack, who retained the ownership until 1914. Both these families are descendants of the famous Sitwell family who still occupy Weston Hall today.

The Courtyard Hall

1914 marked the centenary of the Treaty of Ghent, and thus a century of peace between Britain and the United States since the end of the war in 1812. Plans were made for the celebration of this centenary, many of which had to be abandoned owing to the onset of war. But among the objects achieved was the raising by British subscribers of a sum of £12,000 in order to purchase and restore Sulgrave Manor. The amount paid for the purchase was £8,400. This left insufficient to begin restoration, but after the war a subscription list was opened, which was headed by the name of

The recently created Courtyard, Buttery and Visitor Centre

HM King George V and which raised a further £6,000. With £2,500 given by Americans, the work of restoration, which was entrusted to Sir Reginald Blomfield, R.A. could be begun. A beginning was also made of refurbishing the house, work mainly accomplished by Viscountess Lee of Fareham and Mr. H. Clifford Smith, both members of The Sulgrave Manor Board, the body which became responsible for maintenance and administration of the Manor.

The house was formally opened and dedicated on 21st June, 1921, at a ceremony presided over by the late Marquess of Cambridge, brother of HM Queen Mary. Among the many present was the builder's nearly four-hundred-year-distant successor as Mayor of Northampton. The house has remained open to the

public ever since, but this might not have been possible had it not been for the generous foresight of the National Society of the Colonial Dames of America, a body of ladies descended from the men of the thirteen colonies which formed the original United States.

In 1924 they set themselves the target of $100,000 as a fund to endow the Manor in perpetuity, but this they actually surpassed. To a fund of $112,000 they obtained no fewer than thirty-five thousand subscribers. Thus the Manor was bought by British subscription, restored and refurbished by joint British and American effort and endowed by American subscription. The object of all those involved is summed up in the words of the Marquess of Cambridge at the opening ceremony:

". . . we have had one idea in mind. We want this house to be a shrine for all Americans who visit the old country and a centre from which sentiments of friendship and goodwill between the British and American peoples will forever radiate; and these sentiments we believe to be the greatest security for the world's peace."

A visitor's first view of Sulgrave Manor

The pedigree of the Washington family

(1) Elizabeth Gough = **LAWRENCE WASHINGTON** = (2) Amy Tomson,
                          builder of Sulgrave,   *née* Pargiter
                          born *c.*1500, died 1583/4

Lawrence Washington,   (1) Elizabeth = **ROBERT WASHINGTON** = (2) Anne   Mary Washington = Abel Makepeace
Registrar of the Court   Light   born 1540, died 1619   Fisher
of Chancery

Sir Lawrence Washington,   **LAWRENCE WASHINGTON** = Margaret Butler   Lawrence Makepeace
Registrar of the Court of   born *c.*1568, sold reversion of   bought Sulgrave 1610
Chancery   Sulgrave 1610, died 1616

Sir William   Sir John Washington   **Rev. LAWRENCE WASHINGTON** = Amphyllis   Abel Makepeace
Washington   **M.A., B.D.,** born 1604, died 1652/3   Twigden   sold Sulgrave 1659

Col. Henry Washington   **Col. JOHN WASHINGTON** = Anne Pope
                               born 1632/3, emigrated to
                               Virginia 1656, died 1677

Capt. LAWRENCE WASHINGTON = Mildred Warner
born 1659, died 1697/8

(1) Jane Butler = **Capt. AUGUSTINE WASHINGTON** = (2) Mary Ball
                    born 1692/3, died 1743

General GEORGE WASHINGTON – Martha Custis
born 22 February 1732, died without   *née* Dandridge
issue 14 December 1799

The pedigree of the Washington family

The builders of Sulgrave Manor to George Washington, 1st President of the United States of America.

Commemorative porcelain statuette of George Washington riding his horse, on display in the Deed Room

The House

The shabby farmhouse which was bought in 1914 was smaller than the house that Lawrence Washington built.

The parts which remain of his house are to the south, the porch and screens passage and the Great Hall on the ground floor, the Great Chamber and two smaller rooms above. To-day there is a west wing, containing the Director's quarters, constructed at the restoration completed in 1929. The frontage in Tudor times was considerably wider than it is today. The porch was, as now, central. To the west was the kitchen and buttery, to the east the Great Chamber and more. It is not now possible to tell how far the house extended in either direction, but in 1920 a huge boulder, which could have been a foundation stone, was dug up about fifty feet to the west of the present house, and others were found in a line with the existing frontage. Moreover, the present exterior wall at the east end of the Tudor building will be seen to have been an inside wall. A Tudor pattern fireplace shows itself at first floor level, with, above it, the projecting oak purlins, sawn through between 1700 and 1780 at the time when parts of the house, for reasons unknown, were pulled down. Parts of the Tudor house, which Robert, the builder's son, had enlarged, had already been destroyed by 1700, when John Hodges built the north wing which runs at right angles to the Tudor portion and contains at ground level the Oak Parlour and Great Kitchen and, above, the Chintz and White Bedrooms.

The local limestone of which the house is built is not dissimilar from that of the Cotswold country. The roofs are both stone-tiled, the pitch of the Tudor roof being steeper than that of the north wing. The Elizabethan red-brick chimney stacks are characteristically set at an angle, in contrast with the Queen Anne chimney stacks of solid stone with a projecting base.

The entrance to the house in Tudor times was by the porch at the south. It was added by Lawrence Washington after he had completed his south front, and above the doorway he had placed, in plaster, the royal arms and the initials ER for Elizabeth Regina. Of these arms little more can be seen now than the heraldic supporters, a lion crowned and a dragon, together with a fleur-de-lys and Tudor rose. Above these arms, near the gable, is a triangular device with small

The Manor House from the West, as it was in 1920 before the formal gardens designed by Sir Reginald Blomfield were started, painted on oak from the Manor Estate by Emmie Stewart-Wood RA

birds on either side; and the plasterer, covertly illustrating the source of his own wages, added on the left a lop-eared sheep with falling collar and on the right a lamb wearing an Elizabethan ruff. The sheep, the lamb and the birds have tiny pieces of charcoal for their eyes.

In the spandrels of the doorway were carved the arms of the builder's family, three mullets (stars) and two bars (stripes); not unnaturally, it has been held that here is the origin of the design of the American flag. The arms are to be seen quite clearly in the right hand spandrel. Those in the left were 'differenced' by a crescent beneath the bars, indicating descent from a second son (the builder's grandfather was the second son of Robert Washington of Warton), but they have long been indecipherable.

The South Porch showing the intriguing armorials essayed in pargiting - probably a typical Tudor 'pun' by Lawrence Washington, his second wife's maiden name being Pargiter !

Between the royal arms and the doorway is another representation, in plaster, of the Washington arms, quite modern, and replacing some device the nature of which had become unknown by the eighteenth century. The north courtyard, formed by the Tudor and Queen Anne wings and the gabled end of a building used formerly as a brewhouse and a barn, contains three stone doorways, one leading into the kitchen, one into the Great Hall and one in the south-east corner.

St. James Church, Sulgrave

Sulgrave Church and Village

The fourteenth century church, where the builder of the Manor House and his eldest son lie buried, has much of interest to offer the visitor, including the Washington family pew, now restored, memorial brasses to Lawrence Washington, his wife and eleven children, and marble wall tablets in memory of the Hodges family, who owned the Manor for so long.

The church lies at the western end of this very attractive village, and the houses are mainly of stone and thatch.

The Thatched House

Some of the finest examples are *The Thatched House* immediately facing the entrance drive to the Manor; *Dial House,* a beautiful farmhouse with a stone porch, mullioned windows, sundial on its gable and a datestone bearing the legend 1636.

The Star Inn

The Star Inn is half way down Manor Road, with its tall signpost decorated with wrought iron. *The Corner House* is situated at the junctions of the Helmdon Road, Little Street, Church Lane and School Street, with its datestone in the gable end JCE 1779 and *Rectory Farmhouse* dating from about 1640 is found at the bottom end of Little Street.

Sulgrave Manor Exhibition Rooms

The Eighteenth Century Brewhouse and Dairy now houses the George Washington Exhibition. In a series of displays, tableaux, audio and video presentations, George Washington's career as farmer, soldier and leader, is told in graphic detail. In the loft, the link with the Washingtons of Sulgrave is explained. George's upbringing, education and early career are covered. His experience as a Redcoat fighting the French and Indians in the Seven Years War is dramatically re-created. Marriage and, hoped for, life as a Colonial farmer conclude this part of George's life.

In the first room on the ground floor, the story of George the farmer is told. Explained in a series of illuminated panels that show what it was like to be a Colonial plantation owner, the crops grown, the total dependence on England the mother country for markets, and the gradual disillusionment of George, a Southern Conservative Gentleman, with how he was treated.

George Washington's saddlebags, to be seen in the Deed Room

George Washington's wax seal, to be seen in the Deed Room

Indian chiefs used elaborately carved pipes for smoking. They were called Tabacs, which later gave the name to tobacco

The second room covers the gradual move towards opposition to this treatment and George Washington's role in it, concluding with his appointment as Commander-in-Chief of the American Forces. A nine minute video then takes the visitor graphically through George's career, the successful War of Independence (1776-1782), his election as the First President of America in 1789 and his eight years in office. It concludes with his death at his beloved home at Mount Vernon on 14th December 1799.

Marshall McLuhan, another great North American, once said, *'those who try to make a distinction between education and entertainment, don't know the first thing about either'*.

At Sulgrave both principles are given equal importance.

Education at Sulgrave

Over 11,000 schoolchildren a year now come to the specifically-structured education days at Sulgrave Manor. The quality of our regular presentations and of the *Living History* weeks have created an enviable reputation.

Each *School Day*, the regular education team, in full costume, work with parties of children giving them a full insight into life in Tudor and Stuart times. For two separate weeks each year our *Living History* team bring the whole Manor to life with great accuracy and authenticity. These weeks bring an enthusiastic response from adult visitors and children alike. To see the Great Kitchen up and working, the Great Hall alive with feasting and entertainment and the Bed Chamber active with babies being mothered and wool being spun is a joy to behold !

Functions &
Entertaining

The traditionally timbered
and galleried Courtyard Hall
makes the perfect setting for events
of all kinds.

- Weddings and Receptions
- Celebratory Parties
- Company Seminars
- Club & Society Dinners
- Concerts
- Private Functions